Contents

Who were the Vikings? 4
Viking raiders 6
Vikings in England 8
Viking society 10
Villages and towns 12
Traders and explorers 14
Ships and navigation 16
Viking beliefs 18
Craft, stories and music 20
A day in the life of a Viking child 22
Make a Viking loaf 24
The end of the Viking age 26
Facts and figures 28
Timeline 29
Glossary 30
Further information 31
Index 32

Who were the Vikings?

The Vikings are often seen as raiders and warriors, but they were also farmers, traders and craftworkers. The Viking way of life developed around 700CE and lasted until the 1100s. The Vikings left their mark wherever they settled, and played an important part in the history of Britain.

In the 800s, the Vikings made frequent raids on the British coast. They set fire to churches, stole precious treasures and seized farming land.

Northern raiders

The first Viking people lived in Norway, Sweden and Denmark. But by the 790s, longships full of raiders were setting sail in search of new lands. The Vikings had heard stories of wealthy foreign countries and they wanted to seize some riches for themselves. They were also keen to gain more land for farming.

Explore!

VIKINGS

Jane Bingham

WAYLAND
www.waylandbooks.co.uk

First published in Great Britain in 2015 by Wayland

Copyright © Wayland, 2015

Dewey number 948'.022-dc23
ISBN 978 0 7502 9548 2
Library Ebook 978 0 7502 9555 0

10 9 8 7 6 5 4 3 2 1

MIX
Paper from
responsible sources
FSC® C104740

Wayland
An imprint of Hachette Children's Group
Part of Hodder & Stoughton
Carmelite House
50 Victoria Embankment
London EC4Y 0DZ

An Hachette UK Company
www.hachette.co.uk
www.hachettechildrens.co.uk

Printed in China

Produced for Wayland by
White-Thomson Publishing Ltd
www.wtpub.co.uk

Editor: Izzi Howell
Designer: Ian Winton
Picture researcher: Izzi Howell
Illustrations for step-by-step: Stefan Chabluk
Proofreader: Izzi Howell
Wayland editor: Annabel Stones

Picture acknowledgements:
The author and publisher would like to thank the
following agencies and people for allowing these
pictures to be reproduced:

Cover (top left) Feodalites/Florian Mazel/Wikimedia, (top
right) OlegDoroshin/Shutterstock, (bottom left) Rob Roy/
Wikimedia, (bottom right) rimglow/Thinkstock, (other cover
elements) Tazzina/Thinkstock, Santi0103/Shutterstock,
Kapreski/Thinkstock, Andrey_Kuzmin/Shutterstock; title
page (left) BMJ/Shutterstock, (right) Berig/Wikimedia; p.3
Jeblad/Wikimedia; p.4 Heritage Images/Corbis; p.5 (top)
Arsty/iStock, (bottom) Nachosan/Wikimedia; p.6 Philip
Bird LRPS CPAGB/Shutterstock; p.7 (top) Stefan Chabluk,
(bottom) SinSpinadas/Wikimedia; p.8 Stefano Bianchetti/
Corbis; p.9 (top) Joseph Martin Kronheim/Wikimedia,
(bottom) www.TourNorfolk.co.uk; p.10 jps/Shutterstock;
p.11 (top) Charles & Josette Lenars/Corbis, (bottom) Corbis;
p.12 ckchiu/Shutterstock; p.13 (top) Dendron/iStock,
(bottom) Ted Spiegel/Corbis; p.14 Stefan Chabluk; p.15
(top) Guerber, H. A./Wikimedia, (bottom) BMJ/Shutterstock;
p.16 Boatbuilder/Wikimedia; p.17 (top) Kokhanchikov/
Shutterstock, (bottom) Richard T. Nowitz/Corbis; p.18
L3u/Wikimedia; p.19 (top) Blue Lantern Studio/Corbis,
(bottom) Diego Moreno Delgado/iStock; p.20 Heritage
Images/Corbis; p.21 (top) Berig/Wikimedia, (bottom) Anna
Stasevska/Shutterstock; p.22 Felix Zaska/Corbis; p.23 (left)
Elena Schweitzer/Shutterstock, (right) Volodymyr Burdiak/
Shutterstock; p.24-25 Stefan Chabluk; p.26 Joseph Martin
Kronheim/Wikimedia; p.27 (top) Wikimedia, (bottom)
AndrewJShearer/iStock; p.28 (top) www.TourNorfolk.co.uk,
(bottom) Nachosan/Wikimedia; p.29 Jeblad/Wikimedia; p.31
(top) L3u/Wikimedia, (bottom) SinSpinadas/Wikimedia.

Settlers, traders and explorers

Once the raiders had won new land, they were followed by boatloads of settlers. By the 1000s, there were Viking people living in Britain, France and Russia. Viking traders travelled as far as Constantinople (modern-day Istanbul). Small groups of settlers made their homes in Iceland and Greenland, and a few daring explorers even reached North America!

Most Viking people lived in small villages. This modern reconstruction of a Viking village shows the type of houses that the Vikings built.

How do we know?

The Vikings did not keep written records, but we have plenty of evidence about their way of life. Archaeologists have discovered Viking homes and ships, as well as a wide range of objects, including weapons, jewellery and tools. Some people whose lands were invaded left detailed descriptions of the Vikings, and some Viking legends were written down at the end of the Viking age.

These Viking chess pieces from the Scottish island of Lewis provide useful evidence about Viking costumes.

Viking raiders

The Viking raids on Britain began around 790CE. Over the next hundred years, Viking raiders sailed around Europe, raiding as they went. They launched attacks on places in Britain, France, Spain, Italy and North Africa.

Attacking England

In the 790s, England was a mainly peaceful country, ruled by Anglo-Saxon kings. These Christian kings paid for many churches and monasteries to be built. One of the richest monasteries stood on the island of Lindisfarne, just off the coast of northeast England. In 793, the monastery was raided by Viking warriors who seized its treasures and killed many monks. This was the first of many attacks on English monasteries, villages and towns.

The Vikings left the monastery at Lindisfarne in ruins.

Scotland, Ireland and the Isle of Man

Around the year 800, Viking raiders arrived in the Shetland Islands to the northeast of Scotland. Then they moved south, launching attacks on Scotland and Ireland. The Isle of Man, which lies between northwest England and Ireland, became a Viking kingdom in 1079.

Places where the Vikings settled

This map shows how the Vikings first raided, and then settled in the the British Isles.

Vikings in France

In the early 800s, the Vikings gained control of many towns in the kingdom of the Franks (known today as France). But then the Franks began to fight back. They won back most of their land, except for a northern kingdom which was ruled by a powerful Viking called Rollo. This kingdom became known as Normandy, which means 'the land of the North Men'.

Rollo the Viking was the first Duke of Normandy. He was an ancestor of William the Conqueror who conquered England in 1066.

Vikings in England

I n 865, a large number of ships set out from Denmark to conquer England. These Viking invaders were known in England as the Danes, and their fighting force was called the Great Army.

The Anglo-Saxon people must have been terrified by the sight of the Danish ships arriving on their shores.

Invading England

First, the Danes landed in East Anglia. Then they spread north and west. In 866, they captured York, and went on to control northeast England. In 870, the Great Army moved west and attacked the kingdom of Wessex. It seemed that the Danes would conquer all of England, until the Anglo-Saxons began to fight back.

According to legend, King Alfred visited the Danes in their battle camp disguised as a musician. The information he learned about their plans helped him to defeat the Danes in battle.

Alfred and the Danes

In 871, Alfred became King of Wessex and began to lead attacks on the Danes. Alfred's army defeated the Danes at the Battle of Edington in 878. After this victory, both sides agreed that England should be divided in two. King Alfred ruled western and southern England, while the Danes controlled a large area in the north and east.

Vikings and the Danelaw

The area of England ruled by the Danes became known as the Danelaw, and people living there followed Viking laws. The Danes ruled the Danelaw until 927, when Alfred's grandson Aethelstan beat the Danish army at the Battle of Brunanburh. Aethelstan's descendants were kings of England for the next 80 years, but Viking people continued to live in northeast England.

The Vikings founded many towns and villages in northeast England. This signpost illustrates the Viking origins of the village of South Walsham in Norfolk.

SOUTH WALSHAM

Viking society

Viking society was divided into three main groups. Jarls were warrior lords who owned large areas of land. Karls were free men or women who lived and worked on the jarl's land. Thralls were slaves who worked for the jarls and karls.

Farmers and warriors

In the early Viking period, men usually worked on the land, but they also trained as warriors. In summer, they farmed the land that belonged to their local jarl. In winter, they followed their jarl in raids on foreign lands. The jarl lived in a longhouse at the heart of the village, surrounded by his lands. All the villagers sheltered in the longhouse in times of danger, and they also gathered there for feasts.

This is a reconstruction of a jarl's longhouse. Longhouses were large enough to hold all the villagers if the village was under attack.

Men, women and children

Most Viking men were farmers and fishermen, but some worked as craftsmen, poets and traders. Wives usually stayed at home, but there are records of female carvers and poets. Viking women prepared and cooked the family's meals, looked after their children, and wove colourful clothes and blankets. Children did not go to school. Instead, they worked alongside their parents, learning skills from them.

Viking women wove woollen cloth and made colourful braids. This woman is making a traditional Viking braid, using her toe to hold the end of the braid.

Things and kings

The Vikings held large open-air meetings, known as Things, to decide on laws and punish criminals. The Thing was run by the local jarl, and all the karls and their wives could take part in the discussions. However, by the end of the 900s, the jarls had lost much of their power. Denmark, Norway and Sweden were ruled by kings and the tradition of holding a Thing died out.

Some Viking kings were very powerful. This picture shows King Cnut, who ruled England, Denmark, Norway and Sweden.

Villages and towns

The Vikings hung their fish from wooden racks, so the fish would dry out and last for many months. People in Scandinavia still dry fish like this.

M any Viking villages were built near water, so the villagers could rely on fishing as well as farming. Their houses were grouped around the jarl's hall and surrounded by his land.

Farming and fishing

Farmers grew oats, barley and rye as well as a range of vegetables, such as cabbages, beans and carrots. They also kept cows, sheep, pigs, goats and chickens. People living near rivers caught fish using nets and spears. If they lived near the coast, they hunted seals, walruses and even whales.

Viking homes

Most Viking homes were shared by large family groups, including parents, children and grandparents. Houses were usually rectangular in shape, with benches for sleeping built into the walls. Tools were hung from pegs or ropes, and valuable possessions were stored in wooden chests. There was a stone fireplace in the centre of the house, and all the family cooked, ate, worked and slept in a single, smoky room.

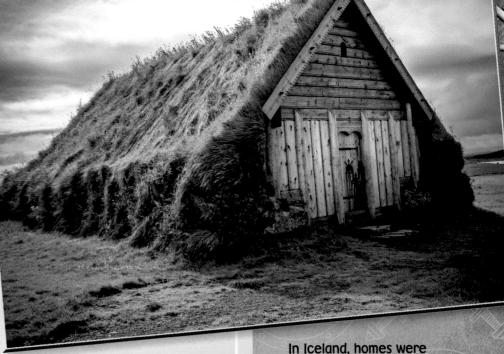

In Iceland, homes were covered by earth and grass to keep them warm inside.

In the 900s, the Vikings started making silver coins for trading. Before that, they bought goods using lumps of silver, known as 'hack silver'.

Traders and towns

By the 900s, the Vikings had set up trading towns where they could meet foreign merchants. Hedeby in Denmark and Birka in Sweden were the largest Viking towns. York and Dublin were important centres in England and Ireland. The Vikings bought silver, wine, spices and jewellery from foreign merchants. In exchange, they sold furs, leather, iron and timber. They also sold objects carved out of ivory from walrus tusks.

Traders and explorers

The Vikings were great travellers. Traders made long journeys to exchange goods with foreign merchants, and explorers set off in search of new lands where their people could settle.

Russia and beyond

Viking traders travelled through Russia by river and set up trading towns along their route. They built up a Russian kingdom, based around the cities of Novgorod and Kiev. Some Viking merchants travelled south though Russia all the way to Constantinople, in modern-day Turkey. A few continued east to trade with Arab merchants in the city of Baghdad, in modern-day Iraq.

As well as sailing around the coast of Europe, the Vikings travelled as far east as Baghdad and as far west as North America.

Greenland

Iceland

Norway

Novgorod

Sweden

Denmark

Russia

Vinland (North America)

Britain

Kiev

Atlantic Ocean

Constantinople

Baghdad

14

Iceland and Greenland

Some daring explorers sailed west from Scandinavia in search of new lands. Many ships were never seen again, but a few returned with reports of new countries. In 874, Ingólfur Arnarson set up a colony in Iceland. In 982, Eric the Red sailed with a group of settlers to southern Greenland. The colony in Iceland was a success but people in Greenland struggled to survive in the cold, rocky landscape.

Boatloads of settlers made the journey west to settle in Iceland and Greenland.

Reaching America

Around the year 1000, Leif Ericsson, one of the sons of Eric the Red, reached North America. He gave the name Vinland to the place he found, which is probably present-day Newfoundland. After this discovery, several groups of settlers travelled to Vinland, but the Viking settlement did not last. The settlers fought with the Native Americans and decided to return to Scandinavia.

Many people believe that Leif Ericcson was the first European to reach North America.

15

Ships and navigation

The Vikings were skilled carpenters and boat-builders. They designed and built a range of boats, including small fishing boats, longships for raiding and cargo ships called knorrs.

Longships and knorrs

Longships were designed to travel fast over stormy seas. They could also sail in shallow water and were narrow enough to travel up rivers. Knorrs were wider and deeper than longships, with a large central storage space. They were used by merchants to transport trading goods. Sometimes, settlers travelled in knorrs, along with all their possessions and even some cows and sheep.

The Roskilde Viking Ship Museum in Denmark displays the remains of several Viking longships. This wooden ship is supported by a metal frame.

Finding their way

The Vikings did not use compasses to help them navigate, but they still managed to find their way across wide oceans. Sailors used the position of the sun, moon and stars to help them plan their route. They studied the movement of winds and ocean currents, and observed the habits of seabirds and fish to help them find their way safely to land.

When Viking sailors believed that they were nearing land, they released some captured birds. Then they sailed behind the birds, as the birds obeyed their instinct to fly towards the land.

Difficult journeys

Most Viking ships had a large, square sail, and a tiller to control their course. They were also equipped with oars, which were used whenever the wind died down. On some river journeys, the river became too shallow or too rocky for the voyage to continue. Then the crew had to carry their boat on their shoulders until they reached the next safe stretch of river.

This man is making a model of a Viking boat. He is working on the tiller - a steering paddle at the back of the boat.

Viking beliefs

In the early Viking age, the Vikings were pagans who worshipped many gods, but in the 700s, Christian missionaries began to convert the Viking people. By the 1000s, most Vikings followed the Christian religion.

Gods and ceremonies

The early Vikings worshipped a range of gods. Odin was the god of war and wisdom, Thor was the god of law and order, and Freya was the goddess of love and death. People gathered to worship in clearings in the woods. They sacrificed animals as gifts for the gods. Sometimes they even performed human sacrifices.

This statue shows the Viking god Thor. People believed that the sound of thunder was made by Thor banging his hammer.

Life after death

In the early Viking age, people believed that warriors went to Valhalla after they died. Valhalla was the feasting hall of the gods, and it was ruled over by Odin. Some warrior kings were buried in ships so they could sail to Valhalla. Burial ships were packed with weapons and other treasures. Dogs, horses and even slave girls were buried with their king.

An artist's view of life in Valhalla

The coming of Christianity

Most Viking people living in England had become Christians by the 900s. After King Alfred the Great defeated the Danish army in 878, he insisted that the leader of the Danes should be baptised as a Christian, and the Viking people followed their leader's example. In the Viking homelands of Norway, Sweden and Denmark, people were slower to accept the new religion. It was not until the 1000s that these countries all had Christian kings.

Vikings in Scandinavia built churches with very steep roofs. Some of these churches still survive today.

Craft, stories and music

The Vikings were expert craftworkers. Blacksmiths made tools, weapons and cooking pots. Wood-turners produced bowls, cups and plates, and leatherworkers made shoes and belts. Some highly skilled workers made luxury goods for kings and nobles.

This wooden ship's prow shows the skill of the Viking carvers.

Metalwork and carving

Skilful metalworkers created fine weapons and jewellery, using silver, gold and precious stones. Wood-carvers decorated buildings, furniture and ships, and stone masons carved scenes on boulders. Antlers, tusks and animal bones were made into chess-pieces, ornaments and combs.

Stories and music

Storytelling was an important part of Viking life. Poet-musicians related the adventures of gods, heroes and monsters in long, exciting tales, known as sagas. The storyteller would strum on his harp as he recited his stories. Other musicians played on pipes and horns.

Scenes from Viking stories were often carved on stones. This carved and painted stone shows battle heroes arriving at Valhalla, the feasting hall of the gods.

Carving runes

There was no Viking alphabet, but carvers used symbols, called runes, which had special meanings. Each rune represented a word, such as 'sun' or 'year'. Runes were carved on memorial stones that marked the graves of kings. They were also carved on the blades of swords. People believed that runes could give a sword magical powers.

This Viking memorial stone has runes running around its border.

A day in the life of a Viking child

This is a fictional account by a Viking girl. She describes a typical day in her life.

Greetings! I am Edda, daughter of Helga and Ulf, and sister of Eric and little Frodi. I live in a village in the east of England.

Each morning I get up at sunrise and milk our family cow. Then I help Mother to cook porridge for our family. Father and Eric are always so hungry! They usually work in the fields all day so we hardly see them.

In the morning, I chop up cabbage and onions for a stew, and take our loaves to be baked in the village oven. Everything takes a long time because I have to make sure that little Frodi doesn't get into trouble.

In the afternoon, we get on with our weaving. I am very proud of the blanket I'm making. Then Father and Eric come home and we settle down to eat – cabbage stew, cheese and bread. Delicious!

After we've eaten, we sit round the fire and tell stories. Eric is always boasting about his battle skills. I show him my weaving but he isn't impressed. He will never admit that I work as hard as he does!

The account of Edda's day has been written for this book. Can you write your own account, by Edda's brother, Eric, or by her best friend, Ingrid, describing their life in the village? Use the facts in this book and in other sources to help you write about Viking village life.

Make a Viking loaf

Viking bread was heavier and coarser than the bread we eat today. People often ate it with homemade butter and cheese or with honey from their beehives. Try making this simple loaf to get an idea of the kind of bread the Vikings ate.

You will need:

460 g wholemeal flour

280 g white flour

1 x 5 ml spoon baking soda

1 x 5 ml spoon salt

75 g rolled oats

500 ml warm water

1 Use a wooden spoon to mix the flour, baking soda, salt and 65 g of the oats in a large mixing bowl. Save 10 g of oats for later.

Stir in the water until the mixture becomes hard to stir. Then use your hands to squash and fold the mixture into a dough. Make sure all the flour is mixed in.

3 Tip the mixture onto a board and shape it into a round loaf. Then place it on a greased baking tray. Sprinkle the rest of the oats on top.

4 Put the bread into a cold oven and turn on the oven to 190°C/gas mark 5. Bake your loaf for one hour. Ask an adult to take the loaf out of the oven. Leave it to cool on a wooden board. Then pull off a chunk to eat, just like the Vikings did!

The end of the Viking age

B y the year 1000, Norway, Sweden and Denmark were independent Viking kingdoms. In France, the descendants of Rollo the Viking controlled Normandy. England became a Viking kingdom in 1013, when King Sweyn Forkbeard of Denmark led a successful invasion and was crowned king of England.

Sweyn and Cnut

Sweyn ruled England for just five weeks before he died and the throne returned to the Anglo-Saxons, but it wasn't long before Sweyn's son, Cnut, invaded England and claimed the throne. Cnut was king of England from 1016 to 1035. During his reign, he also became king of Denmark, Norway and parts of Sweden, making England part of a great Viking empire.

King Cnut was a wise ruler. He taught his followers that he was not all-powerful by showing them that he could not control the sea.

26

The Norman Conquest

After Cnut's death, his sons inherited the English crown, but in 1042, the Anglo-Saxons took control of England again. King Edward the Confessor ruled until 1066, when he died without an heir. The English nobles chose Harold, Earl of Wessex, as their king, but there were two rivals for his crown. Harald Hardrada, King of Norway, invaded northern England and was defeated by Harold. Very soon afterwards, William, Duke of Normandy, invaded southern England and won the Battle of Hastings. Harold was killed in the battle, William became the new king, and the Norman age began.

This scene from the Bayeux Tapestry (made in the 1070s) shows the Norman army sailing to England. You can see the influence of their Viking ancestors on the Normans' ships.

The end of the Vikings

Some people say the Viking age ended in 1066. In fact, the Viking raids continued for the next hundred years, although they were much less frequent than before. In the Viking homelands of Norway, Sweden and Denmark, people gave up their old beliefs and the Viking way of life slowly disappeared.

The Vikings are remembered in many places where they settled. In the Shetland Islands, people hold a winter festival in which they burn a Viking longship.

Facts and figures

English place names ending in 'thorpe', 'sham', 'dale' and 'wick' date back to Viking times. 'Thorpe' means a settlement, 'sham' was a village, 'dale' means a valley and 'wick' was a harbour.

SOUTH WALSHAM

Viking longships were around 30 m long. They could carry up to 80 men and could travel 200 km per day.

Some Viking warriors were extremely fierce. They were known as berserkers and they howled like wolves as they fought. Before a battle, berserkers worked themselves into frenzy and bit down hard on their shields.

Most Viking people did not live beyond the age of 50. Children were considered to be adults by the time they reached the age of 12!

Some Viking words have become part of the English language. 'Sky', 'law', 'die' and 'egg' are all Viking words.

The Vikings loved contests and games. They had skating, swimming and diving contests and they played board games.

Many people think the Vikings wore helmets with horns. In fact, there is no evidence from the Viking age that warriors wore horned helmets. Only one Viking helmet has been discovered and it does not have any horns.

Timeline

700CE   Early Vikings in Scandinavia start building longships.

793   Vikings raid the monastery of Lindisfarne in northeast England.

795   Raids on Scotland and Ireland begin.

830   Raids on the British Isles and France increase.

860   Vikings found a kingdom in Russia.

865   The Danish Great Army lands in England.

874   Vikings settle in Iceland.

878   King Alfred defeats the Danes at the Battle of Edington.

886   England is divided between the English and the Danes.

911   Rollo the Viking gains Normandy.

982   Eric the Red starts to explore Greenland.

1000   Leif Ericsson and his crew reach North America.

1013   Sweyn Forkbeard, king of Denmark, conquers England.

1016   Cnut becomes king of England. He rules until 1035.

1042   Edward the Confessor becomes king of England.

1066   Duke William of Normandy wins the Battle of Hastings and becomes the new English king. The Norman age begins in England.

1100s   The Viking age comes to an end in Scandinavia.

baptise To pour water on a person's head as a sign that they have become a Christian.

CE The letters CE stand for common era. They are used to date years after the birth of Christ.

coarse Rough and lumpy.

colony A region where people have settled, which is controlled by the home country of the settlers.

convert To persuade someone to join a religion.

current The movement of water in one direction.

Danelaw An area or district in east England where people had Danish rulers and followed Danish law.

Danes People who come from Denmark.

descendants People belonging to later generations who all share the same ancestor.

evidence Objects and information that help to prove something.

figurehead ...

heir Someone who will inherit a title, money or property.

inherit To receive a title, money or property from another person after they have died.

tradition A way of behaving that does not need to be taught.

invade To attack a country with the plan of taking it over.

ivory A hard, cream-coloured material made from the tusks of elephants or walruses.

jarl A nobleman in Viking times. Jarls owned land, held feasts and led armies in battle.

karl A freeman in Viking times. Karls farmed jarls' land and fought for him in battle.

longship A long, narrow battle ship with a sail and oars.

missionaries People who persuade others to give up their old beliefs and take up a new religion.

navigate To travel in a boat or other vehicle and find your way to a place.

prow The pointed front of a ship or boat.

reconstruction A model of something that is made to look as similar as possible to the original thing.

relics Parts or pieces of things that belong to ancient times.

Scandinavia A name for the northern countries of Norway, Sweden, Denmark and Finland.

source Something that provides information.

Further reading

Best and Worst Jobs: Anglo Saxon and Viking Times, Clive Gifford (Wayland, 2015)
History Detective Investigates: Vikings, Clare Hibbert (Wayland, 2014)
Viking Life series (Wayland, 2013)
What they don't tell you about: The Vikings, Neil Tonge (Wayland, 2013)

Websites

www.bbc.co.uk/schools/primaryhistory/vikings/
A guide to Viking life, including sections on family life, beliefs and stories and Vikings at sea. Includes an archaeology game called 'Dig it up'.

www.primaryhomeworkhelp.co.uk/vikings.html
An illustrated site for children, including sections on food, clothes and houses.

www.bbc.co.uk/history/ancient/vikings/launch_gms_viking_quest.shtml
An interactive game set in 793. Can you build a ship, cross an ocean, carry out a raid, and return home to claim a prize from your chief?

Index

Æthelstan 9
Alfred 9, 19, 29
Anglo-Saxons 6, 8, 19, 26, 27

berserkers 21
bread 22, 24, 25

carving 11, 20, 21
chesspieces 15, 20
children 11, 16, 22, 23, 25
Christianity 6, 18, 19
churches 4, 6, 19
cloth 22, 23, 24
clothes 17, 20

Danelaw 9
Denmark 4, 5, 11, 13, 14, 19, 26, 27, 29

Dublin 7

England 4, 5, 6, 7, 8, 9, 11, 18, 19, 22, 26, 27, 29
Eric the Red 15, 29

gods and goddesses 16, 18, 21
Germany 8, 29
Greenland 8, 14, 15, 29

helmets 29
houses 5, 10, 12, 16

Iceland 6, 13, 14, 15, 29
Ireland 7, 19, 29
Isle of Man 7
Italy 6
ivory 16

jarls 10, 11, 16
jewellery 6, 16, 20

karls 10, 11
knorrs 16

Leif Ericsson 15, 29
longhouses 10
longships 4, 16, 17, 27, 28, 29

maps 7, 14
missionaries 18
monasteries 6, 19
music 21

Norman soldiers 6, 27, 29
North America 5, 14, 15, 29
Norway 4, 11, 14, 19, 26, 27

raids 4, 5, 6, 7, 10, 16, 27, 29
Rollo the Viking 7, 26, 29
runes 21
Russia 5, 14, 29

sacrifices 18
sagas 21
Scotland 5, 7
Spain 6
Sweden 4, 11, 13, 14, 19, 26, 27
Sweyn Forkbeard 26, 29
swords 21

Things 11
thralls 10
timeline 29
towns 6, 7, 9, 13, 14
trade 4, 5, 11, 13, 14, 15

Valhalla 19, 21
Viking words 28
villages 5, 6, 9, 10, 12, 22, 23

warriors 4, 6, 10, 19, 26, 29
William the Conqueror 7, 27, 29
women 10, 11

wool 5, 18

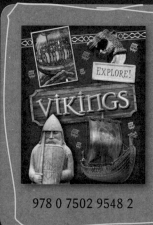